Wise by Nature

Samantha Castro

Cover Art: Nick, DigitalHandArt Studio
www.samanthaecastro.com

Dedicated to my dad, who always encouraged me to be whoever I wanted to be. I will spend the rest of my life attempting to be just like him.

Foreword

Wise by Nature is a collection of poems, prose, personal essays, and literary works from the beginnings of my writing career to my present state. In other words, I hope this is the worst book I release. Don't get me wrong, I am immensely proud of the compilation I'm able to present to you, but I'm self-publishing *Wise by Nature* between the ages of sixteen and seventeen, and I plan on writing until I am unable to do so. I hope this novel is the most inexperienced, error-eroded, grammatically flawed piece of work I ever put into the world because it is my first, and I fully intend on aging, learning, and growing with my craft.

Growing up, I relied on literature, specifically poetry, to get me through some of the worst times within my seventeen years. Naturally, I've spent most of my time attempting to recreate and reimagine some of the most beautiful, soul touching work I've read. *Wise by Nature* follows the journey of my adolescence, through its storms and rainbows, from the view of being wise, but young. Grief, disdain, anger, and sadness are explored in all of their multitudes and individual layers, while being decoded, berated, and explained.

I would like to preface this by noting that many sensitive subjects are touched upon within this narrative, and if you feel compelled, please put the book down at times. The words will always be here when you're ready.

Wise by Nature

"She's wise by nature", my aunt said lightly,
when my mother's suicide attempt didn't kill her,
but me.
Wondering how I was calm when my world was in
flames,
unknowing of abuse I'd delicately consider
"growing pains"
Wise by nature, every time at five I'd sign my name
incorrectly
insisting that Wise was my maiden name, by
heredity.
I'm half of her and she's half of me
which makes me wise by nature, by creed.
Wise by the eyes that my grandfather also held,
the name he gave my mother, the voice with which
she yelled.
Perhaps I'm wine by nature, Almaden boxed
chardonnay.
the sweet voice that put me to sleep, held me while I
lay
proceeds to make me shut down, space out
freak out, cry out, start to shout
with the wise voice I inherited, and I hate the sound.
I hate the way her footsteps have a pound.
but to those who really, really loved her
and believe I'm a mere, angsty teenager,
let's recall when she told me I should take my own
life

when I was eleven, when I was five and she held a knife.
when I was fourteen, and she threw a phone book at my head.
I'd joke about how she missed, and how she's weak, and she wished I was dead.
Yet although my mother didn't leave a mark.
She's the reason for my passion, my purpose, my spark.
the reason I write, somewhat spitefully because in my teens
I became envious of the girls with their mothers I'd seen.
I missed someone who was in my house, right in front of me,
but before she drank, when being wise was who I'd want to be.
Wise by nature, I am instinctively
an old soul because no one took care of me.
Experienced, enlightened,
exploited, frightened.
Wise by nature, wise by curse,
Wise by my lips that hold the same purse.
Wise in face, wise in voice, wise in mind.
Wise is the title of the girl who used to be mine.
Before mom got violent, when mother's day didn't hurt.
I wanted my mom back, she was mine first.
but the seed cannot go back into the fruit

Wise by Nature

when it rots away, you're left with just roots.
but they can't hold you down unless you let it.
She can't kill me if I don't listen and commit.
I can break the cycle if i'm conscious,
and for a Catholic, she's quite pontius.
Wise enough to know better, do better.
It's in my nature.

The are only two northern white rhinos left on the
planet,
a mother and a daughter.
Sometimes I think about her,
when her mom decides to migrate somewhere else
and leave her to fend for herself.
Everyone will be so devastated for her,
but not quite understand,
because people never get these things until they
happen to them.
I hope that baby rhino acts differently than I and
doesn't water a dead plant.
I hope she doesn't blame herself for being the last
of her kind.
I hope she doesn't reminisce about moments like
now, when it's just a mother and a daughter against
the world.
but I hope she's cherishing these moments while
they're here.
I hope she doesn't drink like her mother did.
I'm sorry, for when she loses her mom.
I'm sorry, for when it's only her against the world.
but life will go on, and time will make wounds fade,
and she will survive as a lone rhino
in a world who killed her kind.

Wise by Nature

A letter to Mimi

The girl I was at merely three,
before mom always drank.
Who climbed that one dogwood tree,
before my heart forever sank.
I didn't know the letters I wrote
would haunt me years later.
Something I still can't emote,
how much I miss, but hate her.
"Happy mother's day mommy"
can destroy my psyche.
My eyes erupt a tsunami,
The nature I grew up in drowns me.
from that one dogwood in the yard,
to the storms of my adolescence.
 give me kind regards
after the erosion of my mother, post my pubescence.

Wise by Nature

I begged you not to become a stranger to me,
admiring your every eyelash and skin cell.
You mocked my emotion towards you,
and although I could say no one will ever,
ever love you that much again,
it would be in vain
and that's a trait that I inherited from you.
But like every memory between us,
every word you said
every fight,
the blood, bright red, staining my hands,
it will fade away.
I didn't want you to fade away,
but I can't control human nature.
We're too similar, we're two repelling magnets.
the parts of you I longed for are parts of you I can't
remember anymore,
all you've left me is gratefully devastated.

Falling isn't voluntary, but to get back up is.
It was not my choice to become bewitched,
entranced, enamored with you.
but I chose to leave you after learning this.
I chose myself, because you couldn't choose me.
Someone has to choose me.

I was the person you fell for before I became yours,
so when did my identity become synonymous with
you?
I was mine before I belonged to you.
I am mine, and I will not always belong to you.
and that truth remains.
I am not owed to you,
I belong by choice.
So I will unfriend you and remain in love with you.
I will live, and I will love, and I can be myself.
It doesn't mean I want to, but I can.

Wise by Nature

You're the air forced out of my lungs.
I would die if I kept you inside.
You're an open cut bleeding out,
and I can't stitch myself up.
You're a current flowing away,
and I'd drown if I went with you.
You can kill me, and I'd let you,
but it's not in my nature.

Wise by Nature

How can I ever talk to you?
Because a year ago, I wasn't able to,
and a year prior, it's all I ever did.
You didn't just break my heart,
you found me as I was,
shattered fragments of glass.
a mirror thrown, because my mother hated her
reflection
and you made me into a disco ball.
You took every shattered faction,
you told them you loved them,
and you stepped on them,
leaving me in infinite pieces.

Wise by Nature

A cocoon of my bed, and my room,
and my favorite songs, and books I read.
Held in solitude alone, like the womb
but my mother is long gone,
my physical body developed,
but my soul isn't complete.
Peace and quiet developed my psyche,
my traits, my opinions, my morality.
A butterfly cannot spread her wings in the cocoon,
she will shed the persona of her former self,
and she does it all alone.
I don't need anyone.

Wise by Nature

She likes the songs I do,
We have the same exact tattoo.
But does she laugh at your stupid jokes?
Every time she sees you, does she choke?
Words fail when your eyes meet mine,
every day, still, after all of this time.
and I hate to wreck your home,
but it's 7pm and I'm all alone
and that hasn't happened since I was fourteen.
when the tragic future of ours was unforeseen.
Before pieces of you became the best parts of me.

Wise by Nature

It only takes one match to light a lovebomb
and that you surely did.
Within a few days it felt like you had a chokehold
on me.
Within a few more you decided I wasn't worth the
time,
or even the words for an explanation why.
So I tell myself that I don't need you to survive,
that all you did was waste my precious time,
but deep down, I blame myself every minute.
I regret you all the time for lighting me on fire,
and leaving when you saw ashes in my hair.
I'm mad at you for not accepting me as I am,
for shoving my baggage into me and knocking me
over.

Wise by Nature

I see you in the mirror,
I hear you when I yell.
I feel you when I drink,
maybe that's why I do.
I tried blonde hair to bring me closer to you,
I cut my long hair like you did.
I'm not meant to be you, but my body clings to you.
My soul's umbilical cord is uncut.
You killed me when you killed yourself.
Do you wish you could change things?
What would you change?
Would you change you or me?

Texts Unsent

hey,
i'm sorry.
but i'm not too sorry.
you turned me into a wretched monster,
every explicative you called me is a reflection of
when our hearts merged and you eroded mine.
but i'm sorry that i spoke to you
how you spoke to me.
i'm sorry the pieces of you that became pieces of
me,
were particles of glass.
too weak to give you what you wanted,
but a bitch when you step on them over and over.

Wise by Nature

You weren't just inside of me.
You gutted my girlhood.
You stripped my clothes and my dignity
just because you could.
I was a corpse on an old mattress
who wanted nothing to do with this.
My pleads were ignored
while my thoughts roared,
No
Ow
Stop
Please
It hurts
Let me go
Please
Let me go

The betrayal was deep,
deeper than you ever made it inside of me.
Deeper than my consistent understanding,
that you were going through a lot,
that life is hard,
that people say things they don't mean.
Epidermal, like the excuses I made for you,
like your rationale.
I obviously wanted it,
I was practically begging for you
to violate me,
by the way I dressed in oversized clothing,
by the way I said I'd never date you,
by the way I punched you in the face after you did
it,
and the guy next to you, for "letting it happen".
The most justice I'll ever get from this,
you spending years claiming you'd take my
virginity from me
and then trying to when I called your bluff
is that you'll read this, and instantly call me,
and call me every explicative you know.
You'll say I'm a liar, and a bitch,
but I didn't even say your name,
you just know, deep down,
deeper than my understanding,
deeper than the betrayal,
deeper than you inside of me,

that we both know what we know.

Wise by Nature

I would've been a piece of dust in your castle of
gold
just to live with you.
Reduce myself to mere nothingness
just so I could see what you're up to.
And you couldn't clean to save your own life,
so I'd spend forever there
as a speck of lint,
a mere particle
on your least favorite sweater.

Wise by Nature

No words find my lips in the aftermath.
My pen doesn't dance the same without you.
My voice stays monotone,
The seasons never change.
Like my eyes,
it always rains.
No flowers grow,
no birds sing,
candles don't smell invigorating,
sweets don't taste good.
Home is a foreign land,
recovering from a civil war.
Just desolate, lonely, nothingness.
There is nothing left for me
in a world without you.

Wise by Nature

I'm sorry my poems don't rhyme.
Is that another way you're better than me?
Do you pride yourself on watching me bleed?
Does it turn you on to make me feel small?
You're going to read this book
and assume it's all about you,
and it's almost true.
You're vain enough to assume in two years,
there couldn't have been someone else to amount to
you.
And it's almost true,
no one else amounts to how hard you hit me,
their touch was gentler than you could ever be.
No one else drained all the life from me,
my salted tears weren't meant to make an ocean.
Their decency surprised me.
So it's almost true,
that every time love fucked me over,
it was because of you.

Wise by Nature

She reminds me of me,
the girl who stole my side of the bed.
Does she sleep curled up in you like I slept?
Her hair is the same color mine was.
Does an unstable box dyed blue arouse you?
She has the piercing you told me not to get,
I got it anyway.
Would you still want me if I hadn't changed from
you?
if I listened about my nose ring,
if I didn't let my hair grow out,
if I boxed myself in a capsule of 2019 forever,
Would you seal yourself in it?
we're a shoebox under my bed,
we're texts I never sent,
we're a black and white faded flashback reel.

Wise by Nature

Your eyes are the same, but further lifeless now.
The pitch of your voice changed, but not the sound.
Little pieces of you still linger, I hold them close,
memories of when I loved you most.
Your new haircut is somehow worse,
I didn't know that was possible.
And you still have me beat academically,
even I knew that was probable.
I remember every detail of me and you,
every argument when I cried in my room,
every day when I wore your clothes,
drowning out the world with your cologne.
My hatred for you is known, you make me ill.
Only you could tell it's simply epidermal.
Like my spray tans I had to "fit in", it fades in time.
Still, I've never had you off my mind.
Are you okay, somewhere out there in the world?
I know your heart is fine with some other girl.
Do you think about paper flowers and "I love you"
notes?
Christmas time, under the tree, you'd hold me close.
You've missed so much, but I don't want to catch
you up.
I'm not the girl with whom you once fell in love.
I did that on purpose, I destroyed who you knew
for the chance that someday,
you could meet someone new.
You could walk back in,
 if our time is right again.

I'd forgive,
I'd act like I can forget.

Wise by Nature

A tour of my house, circa 2014
A corner near my room
with the motion detector knocked off,
from when you pushed me into it.
The kitchen
where you told me I was a selfish, stupid bitch
with no friends
and no purpose.
My drawers,
with a bag of granola bars,
water bottles, and your old iphone 4s.
The living room where you threw the phone at me.
The refrigerator with scraps of food and
chardonnay.
The record player of our lullabies that haunt me
The pictures of where you used to love me.
Oregano in a bag on the counter.
I'm eight years old.
I know too much.

Wise by Nature

I want to believe you'll stay again.
Bring back my innocence
and childlike wonder and faith,
let me believe in magical things
like love and forever.

Wise by Nature

My life fell apart
and I built a new one,
but what would've happened if I stayed?
Would you have come back
to rummage through the ashes
and find me?
You're still welcome,
come knock on the stained glass doors
from when you made me bleed
and I'd let you in
without hesitation.

Wise by Nature

The only part of me
that ever intended on wounding you
were the scratches
on your heart and soul
when you tore me away
from you.

I never want to be able to read your mind.

I don't want to know how you really felt.

And once again, we're strangers.
Strangers who shared their lives together for two
years.
Strangers who confided in each other
and sobbed into one another's arms at night
because they found themselves telling this person
things they've never had the comfort or courage to
admit out loud.
Strangers who pass each other
in the same streets they used to walk through
in cold winters
where their hands were the only warmth they had
and Christmas lights sparkled,
like the feeling they had when their bodies and
souls
intertwined into one another.
Strangers who fell dangerously in love
and couldn't run away
until the insanity drove them to self-destruction.
Strangers who thought they would be married
someday.
Strangers who called each other their love of their
life
and now swear they're the epitome
of craziness and every undesirable trait a person can
possess,
regardless of how one day,
many many days ago,

this person was all they desired.
Strangers who know the older version of each other
like the back of their hand
and watch it fade away,
as sharpie scribbles do off of children's hands-
patiently and with great pain in the efforts to
remove it by oneself,
yet painless when left to its natural course,
with little remains of it remaining
for long enough that you begin to question the basis
of its origin.
Strangers who fell in love
and now remain two individuals
whose paths once intersected
and combined
and now remain permanently diverged
forevermore.

You're a chapter of my life who doesn't deserve a
page in my book.
But here you are.

Wise by Nature

I remember years ago
like it just happened.
When my head hit the floor,
and I pleaded for you to get off of me,
like a small creature
begging for mercy from a lion.
You ruthless, cruel leo-born,
you wouldn't stop until I was contained and silent.
Your mane is shedding now.

Wise by Nature

Chronic infidelity

Women are not just clothes you can layer and disregard
when we go out of style.
We are not cereal flavors.
You cannot "eat a little and get bored, and try a different
flavor"
We are not objects of your governing,
no matter how hard you try.
Defiance is life-threatening,
but will you understand,
so is our survival.
So is pregnancy,
so is bending over backwards
so you don't have to lift a finger.
I'll take my chances,
But I shouldn't have to.

Wise by Nature

It's finally over.
Four years of loving you,
but only two where I'd proclaim it
off of abandoned rooftops
and instagram stories.
Four years of what if's
of wondering what you thought,
how you thought.
It's finally over,
but I will spend a lifetime
forgetting.

Wise by Nature

Eye contact

Don't look away
when you see me in a crowded room.
Make dead eye contact,
analyze my shades of green
and remember what cowardly ways you hurt me.
Remember when you turned my eyes red,
remember when you made them cry,
remember when they lit up,
just for you.
I curse your name,
but life will curse you
with the memory of me.

In the same way that I wish we worked that fight
out
and I wish I could accredit my success with you
how I'd liked to,
on stage winning an award someday,
blushing at you in the audience,
holding you at my greatest moments,
I'm glad you have to see me do it without you.
Look at all you lost,
and could've had,
and would've had
if you cared enough.
I'm the most reckless mistake you'll ever make.

Wise by Nature

I hope you still end up in Florida
like you wanted
with that dog named Zach
and those three kids we planned on,
but I hope they're not mine.
I hope your life is magical,
I hope you have the nicest guitars,
the most wonderful wife,
the prettiest sunrises,
a beautiful beach nearby,
I hope the sand never gets in the Jeep you dreamed
of,
And I hope you finally grow up, Peter Pan.
I hope your dreams come true,
and you learned a few lessons,
and you tell your children what you did to me,
as an example of how not to treat people.

Wise by Nature

You're the passing glance in the grocery store
that makes me abandon my cart. You're the familiar
face across a bar
where I don't know if I've drank too much
or if you're real.
You're a distant face I can find in 100,000 at
Madison Square Garden
that makes me question how bad my eyesight really
is.
You're the detail
in my crowded moments
that makes life worthwhile again.

Home has a "me" in it.
I will remake the definition of home,
I will create something bigger than myself.
Home won't always hurt.

Wise by Nature

I can't write philosophy on life
if I haven't experienced it fully yet.
But I can say that finally,
I want to live it all.
I don't crave sleep,
I crave living.
I don't always want to die,
sometimes

Wise by Nature

Clean

Clean of you,
a red wine stained dress
I don't wear.
Clean of us,
out of my bloodstream.
Out of sight,
out of mind,
off my skin.
You're not mine to claim anymore,
and that's okay.

The sweetest phrases I've spoken were in your name,
you've taken up memories, rent free in my brain
And I know that forevermore, I have only myself to blame.
You loved every curvature of my handwriting,
every inch of me without wanting more.
Every smile I formed was yours for citing,
We hurt each other many times, but who's keeping score?
It seems as if you have, and held it against me for years.
Yet I would fall back into your graces again,
You destroyed me, but after you glued me together.
You lit me on fire after knitting me into your favorite sweater.
You abandoned me after finding me in a box in the rain,
but I will grow, I will thrive without your pain.
I just reminisce sometimes, it's not personal.
I hope you're doing well, further than epidermal.
I hope your heart is happier than when I broke it,
And I hope you wear sweaters you knit, and aren't allergic.
I hope you're okay without me,
but that's something I don't want to see.

-do not disturb

Wise by Nature

I was always stuck in this trend of being tired,
and it wasn't growing pains,
but leftover growing pains.
I am tired for the five year old
who had to finish cooking dinner.
The child who cleaned up the cracked wine glasses.
She is tired, her bones ached, and they ache still.

Grief is being proud of graduating high school,
and having an extra ticket.
It's giving it away to someone's sibling and
forgetting that you're supposed to have two people
cheering you on.
Grief is walking across that stage,
and for once, making it about you.
You did this.
You made it.
Grief is going to the grocery store after for a pack of
gum,
and finding her favorite flavor on sale,
and buying it,
and remembering the sound of her voice
and the smell of her perfume.
Grief is eroded into my life.

Wise by Nature

Life will continue in your absence,
in the death, in the ashes,
Life will continue.
Life will inch along, as you're on your last leg
like a poor bug squashed for being seen.
The dawn will greet you as you stay awake
and question and plead with god,
and life will continue.
The only thing that will never change
is that life will go on, despite it all.

Wise by Nature

I will never have girlhood to connect to.
Small lace dresses, frills,
running through fields,
dolls, pink, pinky promises,
tea parties and roses,
I will remember the fear you instilled in me,
the violence,
the smell of wine,
the imprint of your punch,
the way your words tattooed my mind,
I will never have girlhood to connect to,
but to mourn.

Wise by Nature

I would place all the flowers at your grave,
but you're not dead yet,
just gone.
I would've had a beautiful funeral,
in a black dress, greeted our family,
but you're not dead yet,
just gone.
Your picture could've adorned every single room,
your name would run in church bulletins
until our entire town remembered your name,
but you're not dead yet,
just gone.
I have to live with the possibility of the dead,
the dead to me,
coming back and haunting me whenever you please.
Because you're not dead yet,
just gone.

Wise by Nature

Everything that has frozen over was once water,
maybe even a nice cup of steaming tea,
greeting you on your grandmother's patio.
It's that one sip, and the feeling of home.
Every icicle that scratched your car,
or every snowball pelted at you
was once a cup of water,
replenishing you after your first soccer game
when you were five.
Everything that has frozen over and hardened
was once a gentle necessity of water,
and that is the true tragedy of living.

Wise by Nature

Love
It's something I never thought I could write about.
I never thought I had the correct experience.
To this day, I have never known love without
violence.
Everything I have loved has caused me pain,
but I have spent much of my life imagining it.
Love is the Sunday morning sunlight,
how it graces the flowers on the countertop.
It's your baggage, not just being held,
but cradled with the fragility it has,
the gentle touch never put upon you before,
and I haven't flinched in years,
I haven't been reminded of the violence it took
for me to be as gentle
for such a long time.
Love is kindness and thoughtfulness,
and I will know it someday.

It's okay.
It's okay that you've changed.
It's okay that life has different plans for you.
It's okay that your opinions are different now.
It's okay that you've grown.
Remember where your roots are.
Be where your feet are.
It's okay to change,
but you'll always be you.

Poetry isn't meant to be linear,
It's meant to make you feel something.
It's here for every moment.
It's here for your wedding day,
it's here for the birth of your first child,
it's here for the death of your parents,
it's here for the darkness and bitterness of the world.
Poetry is here, it has spent ages here,
it will stay.
Take what you need, leave what you don't.
Poetry is a never ending meal meant to fulfill the
starving hearts.
Don't be bashful, the words will never run out and
die.

Wise by Nature

Sometimes I choose to relive the scream
I let out when I found out
you were gone.
Maybe if I was louder,
you would've heard me on your way to heaven
and turned around to hold me.
Maybe you'd stay back,
or you'd take me with you.
As long as I could be with you.

Gratitude is the biggest lesson I never thought I'd
learn through grief.
Accepting that if I thought about the last day my
dad would walk as a gift instead of a curse,
maybe I'd be a little happier.
My interpretation is the only way I can change
about a terminal illness that will kill my father. It's
not an end of life arrangement, it's a celebration just
because he's here.
It's a reminder of how special every day is,
not because of the impending doom,
but because it hasn't struck yet.
I don't hug him tighter because I fear it's the last
time,
it's because I'm glad I get to hug him right now.
I spend an extra second thanking the universe for
every day I get to live with him
because I know one day,
and one day soon,
it won't be this way anymore.

Wise by Nature

I can't be mad at you
for taking everything from me
if I gave you all of me.
You just accepted what you were gifted,
and what if I was the first gift you got in a while?
What if you disregarded my details,
like the wrapping paper on Christmas Day?
What did you rush to uncover?
What layer of me was most fascinating?
What drove you away?

Wise by Nature

How to cope with your dad's illness

Don't believe it. He's fine.

Play google doctor. It takes 30 years to progress...

Then play mathematician with a side of playing God.

By 2053 I'll be 47, most likely married with growing children of my own. He'll be feeble and older anyways! No big deal.

Get used to random alarms. He takes medication every few hours, and he likes to make them have fun sounds. The sirens at 2am don't help your anxiety, but they help him cope.

Note symptoms as they progress. Remind him to tell his specialist. You'll note them anyways, like when he slurs his words because he's losing muscle movement in his tongue or how he went from an optimist to a pessimist overnight.

Try not to overthink every little symptom. It's impossible, but it's a degenerative disease, and as much as you think otherwise, there's nothing you can do to prevent this.

Let every noise startle you. It could be him falling. It usually is the cat knocking something down, but it might not be.

Start baby proofing the house for your parent- no more throw rugs, they're a fall risk. Rails in the bathrooms, no more bridges in the flooring.

You're the only person he has left in this world. Begin to act like it. Counter his depression by acting like a ray of sunshine.

Make breakfast in bed feel special with his favorite foods instead of disabling because he can't walk to the table anymore.

Remind him that it's a disease of the body, not the mind. He is just as capable as he was five years ago, he just needs some assistance in executing it.

Remind yourself that that was a complete lie, but I selfishly miss him doing the things he loved because they were things I've grown to love, too.

Get excited for an FDA approved cure. Get your heart broken when they say he's too sick for it to work.

Accept his fate.

Accept YOUR fate.

Realize that his memory is fading. He doesn't remember how old you are anymore, but he knows you're his daughter. He forgets your full name sometimes, but it's okay, everyone calls me Sam anyways. He can't play the guitar anymore, and his tremors prevent him from being able to drive, but at least he's alive.

Learn a huge lesson in gratitude. At least he can articulate his thoughts to me today. Someday he won't be able to. Someday he won't be able to barely walk with a walker, he'll be confined to a wheelchair. Be grateful he can still hug you, he can still move sometimes.

Mourn him and his future. My children will know no grandparents. No one will be able to walk me down the aisle. My husband will never know the gentle kindness and phenomenal example of a man that my father is.

Hold his hand when he trips. Hold his hand when he cries. Hold his hand when he's worried about dying.

Never tell him you're worried too. Never tell him how sudden noises startle you. How you say a prayer every time an ambulance passes you on the road. How you pray, he always said desperate people had faith. He can't know you're desperate. He has to think you're as sheltered as he tried to keep you. It'll help him sleep, even though his medication gives him insomnia.

Make things special while you have them. Leave out the "while you had them" for his sake.

Celebrate his birthday because he's still here for this one, don't tell him you're worried he'll die before the next one.

Get matching tattoos at 16, because "why not?" Get them because you're not sure if he'll make it to 18, so it's worth the drive out of state to begin bucket listing.

Forgive him for every mistake he made. He didn't make many, and he is still my hero, but he's human.

Remind him he'll be better soon, maybe this new medication will work. They never do, but hope is integral to his survival.

Be selfish in private. Yell at god for stealing everything that mattered to you. Scream at the sky, beg for a why, and you're met with sunshine. How can someone be sunny at a time like this?

Let some of your bitterness go. While passing a father and daughter, reminisce instead of cry. Easier said than done.

Play the songs he used to play in bands on the living room speakers extra loud, hoping they'll jog his memory. Being crushed when they don't.

Stay strong in public. Never shed a tear because he'll be fine. Even when his own doctor cried, his neurologist is one of his dearest friends for thirty years who can never keep his composure when he watches my dad get sicker. I believe all of my dad's small town is mourning him too, wondering how I've dealt with the cards I've been handed.

I make dark jokes like he did, I try to become him by playing the guitar and listening to 70s rock. I talk about him all the time. I will keep him alive when he is not. I will cherish him while he is here. I will cry when he is not listening, and I will know peace by knowing deep down, he would be so proud of his little girl for surviving.

I'm sorry mom.
I'm sorry this entire book is about you in some way,
and I'm sorry it can't focus on the good in you.
Your electric blue eyes,
how you always wore the same red lipstick
and I hated how it stained my cheeks.
How I wish I could be stained by you
In a loving way.
Your stains are wine, impossible to remove,
unwanted and unloved.
I'm sorry about cursing you out,
my screams to the sky that you never heard
but they cursed you too.
The thunderstorms of footsteps you created.
I know you loved the rain,
but you didn't have to cause it.
I'm sorry you had to raise a child you hate.
I couldn't imagine the toll it took on you,
but I witness it every day.

Wise by Nature

I Have Sinned

"Forgive me father, for I have sinned"
Are powerful words, begging at the knees
Of a celibate man in a white gown
Whom I could confess murder to
And he'd tell me one Hail Mary,
Two apostles creed's, and an our father
And I'll be resolved of my grief.
I never understood the meaning
Of confession, why does it matter
If god is omnipotent,
Omniscient,
Omnipresent,
Doesn't he already know what I did
Why I'm sorry,
If I'm sorry?
What authority does this random man have
To tell me if god actually forgives me,
Why does saying out loud "I'm sorry"
Forgive me.
If murderers say they're sorry, they still deserve the
sentence.
I don't know why I confess at an uncomfortable
alter
Saturday mornings at 9 am
In the church where I had my first kiss,
I hope god forgives me for that one,
I should've done that in my home, not his.

Does he know I'm sorry for eating cheerios during mass when I was six and bored,
The gospel isn't appealing when I can't spell "Jesus" yet
But I liked the stories.
Sometimes I wonder if God is sorry, too.
For saying that Eve was made from Adam's rib,
For instilling that subordinate position upon women.
Does he look at his mother Mary and say, you're below me? You're my rib?
And you should've been forced to birth me at thirteen, I don't care if you wanted to?
Does he confess for the violence he indirectly caused,
The hatred spewed onto his sheep for loving someone of the same gender or for who they identify as,
Does god care that his words are skewed for a hateful narrative,
Were they really skewed, or does that just help me sleep at night knowing God still likes me.
Does God want the gay people to beg for forgiveness for who God designed them to be?
Does God destroy his stained glass windows of devotion if they're a rainbow?
Does god feel sorry for the world we created, the hatred based in his scripture,
Does God exist?

Wise by Nature

Is God mad that sometimes I doubt it?
Forgive me father, for I have sinned,
I have chosen compassion over your word,
Hoping you'll be proud if you're up there,
Hoping I'm doing the right thing if you're not.

Overanalyze the creeks in the floor,
they never change.
Your eyes never have either.
Your face ages,
your hair grows,
your favorite things adapt,
your house is up for sale,
you've grown up and apart,
and one thing stays the same.
I still hate change.

Wise by Nature

An owl sings outside my window,
it's Mother's Day.
The wise old owl shares a song
while I cry over my wise old mom.
It's in my nature, to curse the sky
on Mother's Day, to curse
the instagram posts,
the "best friend" quotes
to envy the life that was stolen from me.
It's in my nature to look for traces of my mom.
She'd pick up dimes and remember my uncle,
she'd look for my aunt in their favorite songs.
I look for her in every piece of life without her.
I find her in the memories I'm making in her
absence,
I find her in linen candles, crystal stores,
nag champa incense, and cheap harem pants.
I find her in the owl singing outside my window.
Happy Mother's Day Mom, a wise woman
who made me wise by nature.

Broken was always a negative word growing up. It was a shattered wine glass I accidentally dropped, erupting screams from the people who raised me. Broken meant change, and the only change I knew was the shift between sobriety and drunkenness, and even that was a routine shift which never changed. As much as I wanted to feel familiar and familial, something needed to be broken. In fact, all of the wine glasses needed to be broken. I needed to change, for the future family I'd have someday.

Broken was the devastating blow of losing people to addiction, whether it was their livelihood they'd never get back or losing their life, I was left broken and in need of breaking. Breaking a cycle, a disease passed down and saturated within my genetic coding. I needed to break something I couldn't see, something innate and immovable, but preventable.

Breaking a generational cycle started off for me, in spite and in healing my inner child from the loudness it took to become quiet, but not silenced. Breaking my anger into bundles of sympathy, letting someone cut me off while driving because maybe their mom had just overdosed and they were going to visit her, and not honking at them because I remember the feeling.

Breaking, but feeling whole. Breaking away from the mold and knowing that I'm the first child to survive, giving my cousins growing up some hope for the future. There's a little four year old girl in me screaming "We did it! We did it! Look at us, we did it! We're okay now, we made it!" She echoes in my mind. We made it, we made it, I made it.

Wise by Nature

When we make eye contact in a crowded room,
do you relive our two years?
Do you roll your eyes
hoping they'll take you back
to the room where we fell in love?
Do you close your eyes
and hold your head
to envision it all clearer?
Do you refuse to meet my eyes
because you'll remember calling them beautiful?

Wise by Nature

Get out.
Of my dreams.
Of my requested dms.
Of me.
Of me that one night,
where I was fourteen
and you were seventeen,
and I went to bed clothed
and woke up
with only you on me.
Get out.

Wise by Nature

Sometimes I crumble my blanket and pillow
into a silhouette of you.
It's why I snooze my alarm,
it's a miniature prayer
for one more moment
with you
in my arms.

Wise by Nature

The burns you inflicted on me
made me soft and gentle.
I don't care if it's not a diamond,
it's authentic and
it's comfort and
it's everything I grew up without
and needed
so desperately.

Wise by Nature

An Ode to April 2022

My mom always taught me to look for the best in everything.
People, memories, and specifically, rainy days.
She wanted to raise me to dance through the rain,
and float paper boats when sewers overflowed. She found beauty in the most painful of times.
She called me Mimi,
because it was short for Sammi,
which was short for Samantha,
which was short for the three middle names she gave me out of indecisiveness.
April marks substance abuse awareness month,
and one year of my mom not being in my life anymore.
Going through the motions of adolescence without a mom has been more difficult than anything I've ever faced,
and finding the beauty through moments with my mom
that landed me in therapy or guidance counselors' offices with a case worker
isn't the easiest way to go about this silent,
unknown, and unspoken grief I've experienced,
and it's easy to resort to anger-
for a while, I did.
Stating that she broke my heart
and various accusations

made it easy for me to detach emotion from the
situation
by assuming all of the pain was in the past,
because she was completely gone,
just still breathing.
Out of sight,
yet never out of mind.
Every rough day
ends in the revelation
that my mom's advice would've made it better,
sipping coffee with her
and playing scrabble,
or even just hearing her say
she loved me.
I stayed angry
and silent,
furious, and bitter at the world,
until I realized,
that's not who I am.
I wasn't raised to be bitter,
and although I was raised painfully,
I was raised to know that this too will pass,
as the rain always does.
But while it is here,
to make the most of a rainy day,
to read a good book with tea
or dance in the worst of rainstorms.
I sat there,
stuck,

wallowing in the rains
that filled my lungs
and drowned me
in my own emotions.
I looked for closure
in every square inch
of the house I was raised in,
rereading the books we read,
looking through old photos,
until i stumbled upon a box one night,
containing the letter above.
It wasn't until that letter that I realized,
under all of the ashes from our explosive
relationship,
there was so much love.
My mom loved me more than anyone ever has,
and had every intention of making it obvious.
she had every intention of being the best mom she
could,
a cheer mom, a girl scout mom,
and more than that, my best friend.
Looking through the pages,
the book came to an abrupt halt

right when my mom's alcoholism became prevalent
and destroyed our relationship.
My mom was taken from me
by the stigma attached
to mental health treatment and therapy
which led her to self medicate.
she was taken by the easier path,
the road of less strife.
She had every intention of being my mom,
but was stolen away from me.
This is something I don't like to speak about,
and a conversation that's uncomfortable.
It never sits right knowing that this was preventable,
if drug addiction was seen as the illness and polluter
it is.
I wish I could give you a happy ending
or any sort of closure,
but there is no pretty string of words I can write
that would make you think positively about this
situation.
I miss my mom an unimaginable amount,
and the grief perseveres
through a seen and unforeseen distance between us,
as long as her love for me was promised to.
Always loving her the most,

the best,
and the "pineappliest",
and forever attempting to dance in the rain with
mud on my boots,
like she wanted me to.

Check on your loved ones. Ask if they're doing
okay. Then ask if they're really doing okay. Make
that phone call. Tell them you love them. Give them
one last hug. Ask for that token piece of advice. Oh,
how I wish I could ask my mother all of the
questions now.

What is Death?

The textbook definition of death is "the action or fact of dying or being killed; the end of the life of a person or organism." Societally, the end of life is defined biologically, when one stops breathing or their heart gives out. It's weird having to speak about my mother in the past tense for multiple reasons, but sometimes it just feels like she's dead. With people I'll never see again, I tell them that my mother died about a year ago, and was never really involved in my childhood. People I know correct my usage of the past tense when describing what she liked, didn't like, loved, how she acted, and who she was, but it makes my blood boil. Half of me, my bones, my blood, is derived from her, but she isn't here anymore. The woman who raised me for six years is gone and can never come back. Doctors have confirmed it, those close to us acknowledge it, but there's no obituary found online. There's no memorial I can visit or a tombstone, and no public "proof" that my mother isn't here anymore. When I speak about it, I usually get stares or harsh glances of judgment, and I'm told I'm insensitive or dramatic. For the six years where my dad practically lived at his job, I was the only person who consistently spent all day, every day with my mother. I grew up knowing every detail about her, from the way she always dyed her hair blonde and wore red MAC lipstick. She preferred flare yoga pants, and I know she'd love how they're trending now. She drank Folgers every morning with milk and two sugars, but stopped because of her high blood pressure and anxiety in 2011. Her favorite color was blue, she loved linen scented candles, and smoked Marlboro ultra lights since she was 16 and living in Jackson Heights with her eight siblings, and she was the seventh. My mom's life ended when she was hospitalized last year for an overdose and experienced permanent, disabling brain damage, but she's still alive.

It's weird having to look at someone and know they're not the same anymore. I can tell by her formerly electric blue eyes, which lost their vibrancy and are never enhanced with Great Big Lash mascara, but only on the top lashes so she doesn't look tired as the day goes on. Her athleisure has retired for hospital-style sweats and her Reeboks have been replaced with grandma-style velcro shoes. She stopped ordering her coffee with milk and two sugars, but gets it black now, and she doesn't care what cigarettes she smokes, as long as she has some. She hasn't watched a housewives rerun in years or fangirled over Bruce Springsteen and lost her gold hoop earrings she wore every day since her sixteenth birthday on August 20th, 1977. She also forgot when her birthday was, when mine

is, and how old I am. She misspells our special
nickname from when I was younger. It was Mimi,
short for Sammi, which she spells with an "i", short
for Samantha. She spells it "m-e-m-e" now, and it's
heartbreaking and frustrating every time she tries to
alter a strong memory like that. It's like recording a
new show over an old VHS tape, it's just never the
same, and you can never get back what you had.
She's mean to my father for being slow because she
forgot he had Parkinson's disease, and she didn't
show up to go prom dress shopping with me. When
I found my dress, I cried alone in a Windsor
dressing room- and not over the $60 dress which
fits fine and is a nice shade of red with sparkles.
The entire point of junior prom is to wear a cute
dress, but one you can upstage next year, so it's
nothing Earth-shattering. I was distraught that my
mom would never see it, but rather this shell of a
woman with brain damage and irregular dopamine
levels due to heavy drug use which manifested itself
into Bipolar 1 disorder. So I sat there, torturing
myself with pictures from almost ten years ago,
from when I had a mom and a dad, and they were
both okay. They were both great, actually. I lived
the perfect life for a toddler, with two loving
parents, a beautiful house, and a well-off family,
until everything came crumbling down. I cried for
the little girl, who had no clue. I remember my mom
talking about prom, and being excited to take

pictures with me and send me off to prom, and I opened Instagram to see a "Happy Birthday, Mom!" post on my timeline. It reminds me how unique my circumstances are, or how some people still have the life I lost.

Sometimes I feel uncomfortable when aspects of my life change, because my mom isn't mentally here to experience them with me. She doesn't know that I'm going to be an English teacher, or that I wrote a book. She loved reading, and I know she'd love that I love writing. She walked out on my life when I was fifteen after isolating herself from me for seven years before, and it hurt for a while knowing that our short interactions while both trying to cook in the kitchen or waiting for the bathroom would never happen again. Addiction is weird like that, because I know she only ever wanted to be a mom, and the best she could be. Sometimes I wonder whether she disconnected from my life in order to protect me. Maybe that just helps me sleep at night, rather than the internalized second option, that I was a horrible daughter who deserved all of her Alamden boxed Chardonnay fueled abuse. Verbal, physical, mental, and I was too young to realize that if my mother says talking about my home life is strictly forbidden and I have to lie about every bruise on my body, then something's really wrong.

Wise by Nature

My mom's emotional, mental, and personality death will never leave me. In some ways, I will never leave my mom's room, when I clutched a suicide note and let out a scream that my voice and soul took weeks to recover from. I can confidently say that she will never be that person again, and it was the end of her life, because my mom doesn't wear mauve lipstick, and gray sweats, smoke whatever cigarettes and obscene amounts of weed every day, and does not favor purple over other colors. She does not listen to Adele for hours every day, but the stranger in her skin does. The woman who resides in her room and the stranger who drinks her coffee black does. Part of me died when my mom did, and I know the woman in my living room would be offended by reading this. 2014 me would be shocked and confused, and my mother would cry, and hold me, but never had the self esteem to apologize. She'd just hold me, and that would be enough for me.

Death societally is when I can't put my mom on my FAFSA. Death to me is when her Facebook is an untouched relic of who she was, memories of us, and the life we shared. It's proof that at one point, the woman sitting in my living room wasn't a stranger, and at one point, the mom I've described and imagined was real, and she loved me. The end of that woman's life has come and gone, and it's difficult to understand. It's difficult to write about. It's difficult to comprehend, but if i simplified this, it wouldn't do my dead mom justice. If I made this easier to read or less complicated, it wouldn't justify how I've felt. I've always questioned my choice of the past tense, and I've never understood how she can be dead but alive, but I know deep down that it's the closest way to describe my circumstances. This is not an easy read that makes you feel fulfilled or inspired at the end, because experiencing this never had a silver lining. There is no pot of gold at the end of grief or death, you just keep existing after someone else's life ends. My dad always said that when he died, he'd be the itch in my pocket or that random tickle in my sleeve. My mother is the dull, stabbing pain in my arthritic knees from years of cheerleading. I exchanged ten years doing what I loved for a lifetime of pain when I walked upstairs. Temporary happiness for a lifetime of sad mother's days' and anger when seeing girls my age with their mothers. I've seen many definitions of grief, but I've always loved the idea that grief is the love we never got to share, or that grieving deeply is to have loved fully. In my entire life, I never have, and now know that I never will love someone the way that I loved my mom, through the abuse and burned bridges. But I will spend my entire life describing it and trying to make sense of the unspeakable and indescribable.

Death is a synonym for the absence or loss of something which creates a hole in you, subsequently called grief. The hole is expected to close after an amount of time, but the dirt beneath us is never quite the same after a tree has grown and blossomed and is then taken out following its death. Its nutrients are sparse and the dirt isn't as compact as the layers before it, and the hole is always slightly there. It remains, as grass and new flowers grow over, perhaps in memorium or as a sign of the times. Death is the moment of loss and the traveling through the space between life and what comes after, whatever that may be. She is gone, and can never come back, but at one point, she was here, and she was all of the beautiful things that life contained and every memory that breaks my heart to think about.

Time is a thief, but death is a trap of quicksand that punishes us for loving and assuming any future, teaching us that nothing is guaranteed and everything is a blessing. Death is real, devastating, natural, inevitable, and most of all, complex.

Printed in the USA
CPSIA information can be obtained
at www.ICGtesting.com
LVHW022300161023
761300LV00004B/14